BLOOD SUGAR

Quinoa & healthy living

My everyday recipes from the
Blood Sugar series

BLOOD SUGAR

Quinoa & healthy living

My everyday recipes from the
Blood Sugar series

NEW
HOLLAND

Michael Moore

contents

Introduction

This book has been written with what you, the public, have been asking for. During my travels promoting a healthy living message, it became clear to me that the majority of people who buy my books love great food and entertaining and that there is a growing demand for simple, tasty, healthy recipes for everyday living. I also discovered an explosion in popularity of the superfood, quinoa. So with this in mind I decided to combine the most popular recipes from my Blood Sugar books with some brand new delicious quinoa recipes presented in a handy 'kitchen companion' style book for everyday use.

I love that my books have inspired people to cook delicious food with a healthy approach. Enjoy!

Quinoa
What is it

Quinoa is a seed (but is usually referred to as a grain) grown primarily in South America where it has been a staple in the diet there for many centuries.

Recently, quinoa has become one of the hottest products on the market for its high protein content and low glycemic index.

But for me, it is its versatility that makes it so special. It can be used in many different dishes, savoury or sweet. And it is an amazing substitute for other high carbohydrate products such as bread, rice or pasta, which makes quinoa the perfect ingredient for the diabetic or low GI, high-protein diet that I live on.

Yet, despite its high popularity, many people have yet to taste this special grain, or enjoy its many health benefits.

I was firstly introduced to quinoa about seven years ago in a health bar cafe on a research trip in the USA.

I ate a fantastic fish curry that was served with steamed quinoa rather than rice—it not only tasted great, it was light to eat and left an amazing feeling in my body afterwards. I didn't experience that heavy feeling I can get from eating too much starchy white rice. From that moment on, I wanted to know more about quinoa; the different varieties and different uses.

In fact, I was soon learning more about other types of ancient grains including buckwheat, amaranth, farrow wheat, barley and now, more recently, seeds such as chia and sunflower.

WHITE QUINOA

This is the cheapest and most readily available type of quinoa. It is often the first quinoa that people will taste or use. Light and fluffy when cooked, it is an easy substitute for other starches.

White quinoa is softer in texture and will absorb flavours more easily that the other varieties types. This makes it perfect for use in breakfast and brunch dishes as well as being great in desserts. You will find white quinoa is readily available in supermarkets and health food stores.

The Carbohydrate Exchange

You will notice that most of the recipes in this book have a number next to them. This is the recipe's carbohydrate exchange number, calculated from all its ingredients.

It is only really relevant to diabetics, especially people with type 1 or insulin dependant type 2. These people need to be aware of the carbohydrate exchange number in a meal or a dish in order for them to work out the correct amount of insulin to administer.

They will need to work out how their own bodies process the carbohydrate and balance that with the correct amount of insulin. This should be done with their doctor. This can be a tiresome, but necessary, process for insulin dependent diabetics.

I am very happy that my recipes all have a low exchange number. I really hope that by including this information it helps them enjoy the food in this book with confidence

We have calculated: **ONE CARBOHYDRATE EXCHANGE EQUALS 15 grams or ½ oz of carbohydrate**

This is sometimes called one carbohydrate choice.

RED QUINOA

Red is quite different in texture to white, once it has been cooked. It holds its shape and structure far better than white quinoa and I think red has more flavour. It is my favourite quinoa variety to use on a regular basis—I love the way it retains a slight chewiness. I sprinkle red quinoa over poached eggs or add it to scrambled eggs for breakfast. It's great sprinkled onto salads to give them more bulk or stirred into soups to thicken them. You will find red quinoa is also readily available in supermarkets and health food stores.

BLACK QUINOA

This is more difficult to find but well worth it. I use black quinoa on my restaurant menus for its amazing texture and beautiful black colour, it really is a visual treat. The texture is much firmer and it takes much longer to cook. It will retain its own integrity even when cooked in sauces or wet dishes. I like to use it in dressings and vinaigrettes served with grilled fish.

Such is black quinoa's versatility, it is even delicious stirred into a dish of braised beef or even a classic Italian Osso Bucco. Black quinoa is most likely to be found in health food shops or in a high-end delicatessen.

How to cook quinoa

The main method for cooking all three types of quinoa is to bring lightly salted water to the boil, sprinkle in the quinoa and cook until tender.

Many chefs will recommend the absorption method with a 1 to 2 ratio of quinoa to water. Personally I find that quinoa will sometimes absorb more water and can easily boil dry while you wait for the water to absorb.

I like to cook quinoa in plenty of water, keeping it at a nice rolling simmer, until it is perfectly cooked. Then I drain the quinoa through a fine sieve and refresh under cold water. This gives me perfectly cooked quinoa every time.

WHITE QUINOA will cook in about 12 minutes and will absorb a lot of water. Take care to keep it topped up with boiling water from the kettle. The seed will swell and burst as it is cooked and will look fluffy.

RED QUINOA will cook in about 14 minutes and will be firmer when cooked. Red quinoa will burst and look like small 'worms' when cooked.

BLACK QUINOA will take up to 18 minutes to cook. It will remain largely intact even when cooked. There will be more evaporation during the cooking process so I like to keep the water level high.

Yield

1 cup of dry white or red quinoa will make approximately 3 cups of cooked quinoa

1 cup of black quinoa will make approximately 2 cups of cooked quinoa

BREAKFAST

stone-ground muesli hot cakes

These are filling and a much healthier way of eating pancakes.

2 oz (60 g) self-rising/self-raising flour
2 oz (60 g) stone-ground whole-wheat flour
¼ teaspoon baking soda/bicarbonate of soda
½ cup whole rolled oats
2 tablespoons slivered almonds
1 tablespoon LSA (ground linseeds, sunflower
    seeds and almonds)
1 tablespoon agave syrup
2 eggs
9 fl oz (250 ml) low-fat milk
cooking spray

VANILLA YOGHURT
9 fl oz (250 ml) low-fat natural yoghurt
2 tablespoons agave syrup
1 vanilla bean, split lengthways

RASPBERRY CRUSH
5 oz (150 g) raspberries
1 teaspoon agave syrup

COMBINE FLOURS, baking soda, oats, almonds and LSA in a large bowl and make a well in the centre. In a separate bowl, whisk together the agave, eggs and milk. Pour this into the dry ingredients. Mix until combined. The batter should be the consistency of double cream. Set aside for 30 minutes.

MEANWHILE, mix yoghurt and agave syrup together. Scrape seeds from vanilla bean and stir into the yoghurt. Refrigerate until needed.

PLACE HALF THE RASPBERRIES into a bowl with the agave and crush with a fork until broken down. Stir in remaining raspberries and set aside.

HEAT a non-stick frying pan and spray with cooking spray. Ladle spoonfuls of pancake batter into pan and cook for about 1 minute, or until bubbles appear on the surface of the pancake. Turn over and cook a further 45–60 seconds. Turn onto a plate and repeat with remaining batter.

SERVE PANCAKES WITH raspberry crush and a spoonful of vanilla yoghurt.

Serves 6

MY simple figs on toast with ricotta

4 slices seeded bread

3½ oz (100 g) low-fat ricotta (or see recipe
page 31)

2 ripe black figs (or fresh raspberries or
strawberries)

1 teaspoon agave syrup

TOAST THE BREAD then mash the ricotta onto it using the back of a fork. Slice the figs and also mash them onto the ricotta.

DRIZZLE with a little agave syrup and enjoy with coffee or tea.

Serves 4

Blueberry and tofu protein Shake

This is a high protein start to the day, great after a walk or swim.

3 oz (90 g) silken/soft tofu
½ cup fresh or frozen blueberries
1 banana
1 tablespoon agave syrup
2 tablespoons unprocessed bran
2 egg whites (optional)

3 cups chilled low-fat milk
2 teaspoons chia seeds

COMBINE ALL INGREDIENTS, except chia seeds, into a blender and pulse until smooth.

STIR in the chia seeds then serve immediately in large chilled glasses.

GARNISH with some berries.

Serves 4

CHEF'S NOTE: *You can buy chia seeds from health food shops and many supermarkets.*

Chilled apple, pear & quinoa porridge with raw almonds

One of my favorite breakfast dishes. A little goes a long way. Feel free to add seasonal berries or fruit of your choice.

12 fl oz (355 ml) skim milk
4 fl oz (120 ml) water
4 oz (120 g) white quinoa
4 oz (120 g) plain yoghurt
1 tablespoon agave syrup
1 red apple
1 green pear

pinch ground ginger
pinch ground cinnamon
2 oz (60 g) raw almonds, skin on, finely sliced

PLACE MILK, water and quinoa in a small saucepan, bring to the boil, and reduce to a simmer and cover. Cook, stirring occasionally, for approximately 15 minutes until soft, then allow to cool.

PLACE COOKED QUINOA in a mixing bowl and stir in the yoghurt and agave syrup. Using a coarse cheese grater, grate the apple and pear into the bowl, including any of the juice.

MIX TOGETHER WELL. Add the spices to taste and adjust consistency with a splash of milk.

PLACE INTO small serving bowls and sprinkle with the chopped almonds.

Serves 4

Rainy day hot milk & barley porridge

This is a lower GI version of traditional oat porridge, and is perfect for winter mornings. You'll find flaked barley in supermarkets and at food markets.

16 fl oz (475 ml) milk (2% fat)
2 tablespoons agave syrup
1 cinnamon quill
1 vanilla bean or teaspoon of vanilla essence
1 tablespoon sultanas
3 oz (90 g) rolled barley flakes
2 tablespoons sunflower seeds

2 tablespoons pepitas/pumpkin seeds
2 tablespoons flaked almonds
pinch ground nutmeg

IN A MEDIUM-SIZED SAUCEPAN, heat 12 fl oz (350 ml) of milk with the agave syrup, cinnamon quill and the split vanilla bean or essence. Stir in the sultanas and the barley flakes and cook over a low heat for 10 minutes, stirring until thick and the barley is soft.

IN A PREHEATED, non-stick frying pan toast the sunflower seeds, pepitas and flaked almonds until light brown. Allow to cool, then add to the porridge.

TO SERVE, bring the remaining milk to the boil, whisking to make as much froth as possible (I use my coffee machine steamer to do this). Spoon the porridge into serving bowls, spoon some of the hot milk froth on top and dust with the ground nutmeg.

Serves 4

POaChed red fruit salad

6 fl oz (180 ml) water
2 oz (60 g) agave syrup
1 small knob fresh ginger, grated
1 small bunch rhubarb
9 oz (250 g strawberries
4 fresh black figs
2 oz (60 g) organic red or white quinoa

12 fl oz (350 ml) water
½ bunch fresh mint

PREHEAT THE OVEN to 350°F (150°C). In a small saucepan heat water and dissolve the agave syrup. Add grated ginger. Using a vegetable peeler, peel the rhubarb and cut into 1 in (3 cm) batons. Place the rhubarb into the saucepan with the agave liquid and cook on a low heat for approximately 2 minutes.

TRIM THE STALKS from the strawberries. Cut the figs and strawberries in half and place them into an ovenproof dish. Pour the hot poached rhubarb and liquid over them. Place the dish into the oven for 5 minutes, remove and allow to cool in the liquid.

PLACE THE QUINOA in a small saucepan and cover with water. Bring to the boil and simmer for 15 minutes until plumped and tender, then drain and rinse under cold water.

DRAIN THE LIQUID from the fruit and add it to the cooked quinoa with the finely chopped mint leaves.

ARRANGE THE FRUIT on serving dishes and spoon the sweetened quinoa on the top.

Serves 4

soft-boiled egg dippers with potato hash & salt beef

This is a great protein boost, especially for kids. The dish is also good with shaved ham or turkey.

6 oz (175 g) piece brined beef silverside
  or brisket
¼ small white cabbage, finely shredded
sea salt and pepper
1 tablespoon white vinegar
½ medium onion
½ medium potato (Nicola)

½ medium sweet potato
1 fl oz (30 ml) vegetable oil
8 large eggs, at room temperature
whole-wheat toast, to serve (not included in carb
  exchange)

COOK THE SILVERSIDE in a pot of lightly salted simmering water until tender for approximately 1 hour. Test by piercing with a small skewer. It should slide through the meat with no resistance. Remove from heat and allow beef to cool in the liquid. Once cool, use a fork to shred finely.

COOK THE CABBAGE in a small pan just covered with cold water, a pinch of salt and the white vinegar. Bring to the boil and simmer until tender. Drain in a colander and set aside.

GRATE THE ONION AND POTATOES Into a bowl. Heat a medium-sized non-stick frying pan, add the vegetable oil and fry the potato and onion mixture for 10 minutes stirring frequently. Once the potato is tender add the drained cabbage and finely shredded salt beef. Continue to cook for a further 5 minutes.

PLACE the eggs into a small pot of cold water and bring to the boil. Simmer for 4 minutes for runny eggs and 5 minutes for medium. Remove from the heat and place into egg cups for serving.

CUT THE TOPS OFF the eggs and spoon as much of the cooked hash as you can onto each of them.

Serves 4

greek yoghurt parfait cups

1 tablespoon unprocessed bran

10 oz (300 g) natural low-fat Greek yoghurt

1 tablespoon quinoa flakes

3½ fl oz (100 ml) grape juice or apple juice

1 tablespoon agave syrup

9 fl oz (250 ml) water

1 red apple

4 oz (125 g) fresh blueberries

4 oz (125 g) fresh raspberries

IN A SMALL BOWL mix together the bran, yoghurt, quinoa flakes and grape juice, then place in the fridge.

IN A SMALL SAUCEPAN heat the agave syrup with water. Peel and deseed the apple then cut it into 8 wedges. Poach these apples over a simmering heat for 10 minutes until soft and tender. Add the blueberries and raspberries, remove from the heat and allow fruit to cool in the liquid.

REMOVE FRUIT from the saucepan using a slotted spoon and layer alternately with the yoghurt mixture into serving glasses. Place in the fridge to cool before serving.

Serves 4

Soft & chewy breakfast bars

My kids love these bars—they don't take them to school because of the nuts, but they are easy to make for a weekend or after-school treat.

4 oz (120 g) barley oat flakes
2 wheat breakfast cereal biscuits such as Vitabrits
    or Weet-Bix/Weetabix
2 oz (60 g) pepitas/pumpkin seeds
2 oz (60 g) pistachio nuts, chopped
2 oz (60 g) sunflower seeds
1 oz (30 g) white sesame seeds
1 oz (30 g) millet

1 oz (30 g) flax seeds/linseeds
1 oz (30 g) chia seeds
2 oz (60 g) dried cranberries, chopped
pinch dried ginger
pinch ground cinnamon
3 oz (90 g) butter
3 oz (90 g) agave syrup
3 oz (90 g) honey

PREHEAT THE OVEN to 360°F (180°C) degrees. In a large mixing bowl combine all dry ingredients, mix well.

IN A SMALL SAUCEPAN melt the butter, agave syrup and the honey. Pour this over the dry ingredients and stir, thoroughly coating the dry ingredients.

LINE A BAKING TRAY with greaseproof paper and spray it lightly with oil. Pour mixture in and lightly flatten using the palm of your hand.

PLACE TRAY IN OVEN and bake for 25 minutes, remove and allow to cool for 2 minutes in the tray. Using a large kitchen knife mark cut lines approximately 3 x 1 in (18 x 3 cm) wide. Place in refrigerator until set.

ONCE SET, break or cut bars into pieces and store in an airtight container for up to 3 weeks.

Makes 12 bars

Eloise

Homemade ricotta

2 pints (1.2 litres) full cream milk
1 pint (600 ml) buttermilk
1 pint (600 ml) light cream
large pinch sea salt
1 lemon, juiced

PLACE A LARGE STRAINER over a large mixing bowl and cover it with a piece of fine muslin or cheesecloth. In a large heavy-based saucepan mix the milk, buttermilk and cream together. Place on a medium heat and, continually stirring, gradually bring up to a slow rolling boil, or 345°F (175°C).

ADD A PINCH OF SALT and stir in the lemon juice. Continue to stir until the curds and whey separate. This occurs quickly, so as soon as this happens remove pan from heat and gently stir for a minute.

CAREFULLY POUR all of the contents into the strainer and allow to drain until all the liquid (whey) has collected in the bowl. The curds (cheese) should be firm to touch. Place in a separate bowl in the fridge to cool. Keeps in the fridge for 5 days.

CHEF'S NOTE: *Reserve whey liquid to use in making bread or pizza bases. It can also be reused to make a sharper ricotta by adding more milk and rennet.*

Makes 12 serves

Hot smoked salmon & sweet potato omelette

This is full of flavor and goodness, and being low GI, it will fill you up. For me it's a win all round!

2 medium-sized sweet potatoes
sea salt and pepper
2 oz (60 g) butter
½ bunch continental parsley, chopped
juice of ½ lemon, plus extra to serve
10 oz (300 g) hot smoked salmon
    or ocean trout

6 large eggs
6 egg whites
1 fl oz (30 ml) olive oil
optional: sourdough or wholegrain bread,
    toasted, (not included in carb exchange)

WASH AND PEEL the sweet potato and, using a coarse cheese grater, grate into a bowl. Season with a little salt and pepper.

HEAT a medium-sized non-stick pan, melt the butter and add the sweet potato. Cook slowly over a medium heat for 10 minutes until soft and cooked through. Stir in the chopped parsley and a squeeze of the lemon juice.

PICK THROUGH the smoked salmon to remove any skin or small bones. Using your fingers, flake salmon into a bowl. Set aside.

IN A SEPARATE BOWL, mix the whole eggs and egg whites thoroughly, add a pinch of sea salt and some fresh ground pepper.

HEAT a small non-stick frying pan and spray or wipe with a small amount of olive oil on a paper towel. Add a ladle of the egg mix to the pan and cook to form each omelette. Add some of the hot sweet potato mixture to the centre of the omelette and flake some of the salmon on the top.

USING THE BACK OF A FORK flip half over and roll into a tube. Place each omelette onto a serving plate and serve with lemon wedges or slices and toasted grainy or sourdough bread.

Serves 4

Chickpea & corn fritters with bacon & avocado

This is a filling and nourishing breakfast. I often cook fritters in advance and pop them into the kids' lunch box.

1 medium brown onion
1 fl oz (30 ml) vegetable oil
sea salt and pepper
1 tablespoon sumac (Middle Eastern spice)
4 rashers bacon
4 oz (120 g) full-cream ricotta (or see recipe page 31)
3 eggs

6 fl oz (175 ml) milk (2% fat)
4 oz (120 g) stone-ground wholemeal flour
½ teaspoon baking soda/bicarbonate of soda
10 oz (300 g) chickpeas/garbanzo beans, cooked washed and drained
6 oz (175 g) canned sweet corn kernels, drained
1 ripe avocado, peeled and stone removed
juice of ½ lemon

PREHEAT THE OVEN to 360°F (180°C). Peel the onion and cut into 8 wedges, drizzle with a little oil then season with sea salt and pepper. Cook in the oven for 20 minutes until soft and golden. Remove from oven and sprinkle with sumac. Keep warm.

GRILL THE BACON in a hot pan or on a barbecue plate until crispy.

IN A SMALL BOWL mix the ricotta with a small whisk until smooth. Add the eggs and milk and whisk together briskly. Gradually add the flour and baking soda to form a batter; it should be quite thick.

ROUGHLY CHOP half of the chickpeas and mix both the chopped and whole chickpeas into the batter. Add the corn to the batter and season with a pinch of salt and pepper.

IN ANOTHER BOWL mash the avocado with the back of a fork until broken down, season with sea salt and pepper and juice of half a lemon.

HEAT a small non-stick frying pan, spray with a little oil and spoon in the batter. Add small fritters, approximately 3in (8cm) in diameter, and cook over a medium heat for 3–4 minutes each side.

SERVE on a warm plate with the avocado, the roasted onions and the hot rashers of bacon.

Makes 8 fritters

Apple and almond dutchie pancakes

2 large free range eggs
1½ cups buttermilk
½ teaspoon vanilla paste
2 tablespoons agave syrup
9 oz (250 g) almond meal
½ teaspoon baking soda/bicarbonate of soda
9 oz (250 g) quinoa flour

1 green apple, grated with skin on
olive oil spray, for frying
½ cup natural yoghurt
½ cup whole almonds, finely sliced with
   the skin on
1 tablespoon agave syrup

IN A MIXING BOWL whisk the eggs with the buttermilk, vanilla and agave syrup.

ADD THE ALMOND MEAL, baking soda and the quinoa flour to form a thick batter.

ADD THE GRATED APPLE and stir through.

PREHEAT your pancake griddle plate or waffle iron, spray with a little oil and spoon on your mixture, cook until light brown on both sides.

SERVE with some natural yoghurt and sliced almonds and drizzle with a little agave syrup.

Serves 6

CHEF'S NOTE: *A delicious breakfast treat with higher protein than regular pancakes.*

Field mushroom, bacon & cheese quinoa bake

8 large free range eggs

3 fl oz (90 ml) light cream

6 oz (180 g) full-cream ricotta
   (or see recipe page 31)

3 oz (90 g) parmesan cheese (grated)

3 oz (90 g) cheddar cheese (grated)

1 tablespoon olive oil

1 tablespoon butter

1 clove garlic, sliced

4 large rashers of bacon

1 lb (500 g) field mushroom caps, cut in wedges

9 oz (250 g) cooked red quinoa

9 oz (250 g) cooked white quinoa

sea salt and pepper

9 oz (250 g) pickled red chillies (see recipe
   page 59)

IN A MEDIUM-SIZED mixing bowl, whisk together the eggs, cream and the cheeses.

PREHEAT the oven to 350°F (180°C).

IN A HOT ROASTING TRAY melt the oil and butter together. Add the garlic and rashers of bacon and place the tray in the oven for 5 minutes. Add the mushroom wedges and bake in the oven for a further 15 minutes.

PLACE THE MUSHROOM mixture into a pie dish and sprinkle with the cooked quinoa.

SEASON with sea salt and black pepper. Pour over the egg mixture and bake in the oven for 15 minutes.

SERVE warm or cold with some of the pickled red chillies on the side or a salad of arugula and tomatoes.

Serves 6

quinoa rumbled eggs

You can modify this recipe however you like—I find roasted red peppers with crumbled fetta cheese also tastes great.

8 large free range eggs
½ cup (4 fl oz/125 ml) light cream
sea salt and pepper
2 tablespoon olive oil
1 medium-sized green zucchini/courgette,
    1 cm (¼ in) dice with skin on
1 small red onion, finely diced
1 clove garlic, crushed

¼ teaspoon dried chilli flakes
2 oz (60 g) yellow grape tomatoes, halved
2 oz (60 g) red cherry tomatoes, halved
1 bunch fresh basil, leaves picked and shredded
9 oz (250 g) cooked red quinoa
2 tablespoons pine nuts, toasted

IN A MEDIUM-SIZED BOWL crack the eggs and lightly whisk together with the light cream, sea salt and pepper.

WARM the olive oil in a large non-stick frying pan, add the diced zucchini, red onion, crushed garlic and the chilli flakes. Cook together for 3 minutes.

ADD the tomatoes, basil and the cooked quinoa and cook for a further 2 minutes.

OVER A HIGH heat, add the egg mixture and stir with a wooden spoon or spatula. Keep stirring until mixture just begins to thicken. Remove from the heat and adjust seasoning and chilli level.

SPOON into your serving dishes and sprinkle with toasted pine nuts.

Serves 6

Banana and berry iced smoothie

This is an iced breakfast treat. Use ripe fruit.

3 large ripe bananas, peeled and sliced
juice and zest of ½ lemon
1 tablespoon agave syrup
9 fl oz (250 ml) non-fat natural yoghurt
9 fl oz (250 ml) low-fat milk
9 oz (250 g) bran
5 oz (150 g) raspberries

BLEND BANANAS with lemon, agave, yoghurt, milk and bran until smooth. Pour into a deep dish. Cover with plastic wrap and freeze for about 2 hours or until semi-frozen.

TO SERVE, spoon balls of banana mixture and layer in tall glasses. Top with fresh raspberries; serve immediately.

Serves 4

Thick & spicy-sweet sunflower butter

This paste is a healthy nut-free alternative to peanut butter.

10 oz (300 g) sunflower seeds
1 tablespoon light olive oil
pinch ground ginger
pinch ground cinnamon
½ teaspoon vanilla bean paste
1 tablespoon agave syrup

PREHEAT THE OVEN to 360°F (180°C). Place sunflower seeds on a small baking tray lined with greaseproof paper and place in the oven for 6–8 minutes until toasted but not dark brown. Remove seeds from the oven and allow to cool.

ONCE AT ROOM TEMPERATURE place the sunflower seeds in a blender or food processor and chop to a fine crumb. This will take approximately 5–10 minutes depending on the power of your blender.

ADD remaining ingredients to sunflower crumb and continue to blend until a smooth paste is formed. This may take a while. Adjust sweetness and spices to your own taste.

REMOVE and store in a clean, tightly sealed jar.

Makes 1 large jar, or approximately 24 serves

LIGHT MEALS
& SNACKS

mozzarella with red quinoa & black cabbage

I love this salad with a simple roasted chicken.

4 vine-ripened truss tomatoes
sea salt and pepper
1 bunch black cabbage (cavalero nero)
1 clove garlic
2 tablespoons red wine cabernet vinegar
2 small French eschalots/shallots
2 fl oz (60 ml) olive oil

1 lemon, zest and juice
pinch dried chilli flakes
9 oz (250 g) cooked red quinoa
2 balls fresh mozzarella
1 head of red endive
1 bunch baby basil leaves

PLUNGE THE TOMATOES into boiling water for 20 seconds then place into ice cold water immediately. Peel the skin away from the tomatoes.

PAT THE TOMATOES dry and slice them approximately 1 cm (¼ in) thick. Season them with some salt and pepper and allow to sit at room temperature.

WASH AND DRY the black cabbage then shred it finely with a large sharp knife.

IN A MIXING BOWL, place the garlic, cabernet vinegar and eschalots with the olive oil and the lemon zest and juice. Leave to stand for 10 minutes then add the shredded cabbage and chilli flakes and stir well. Leave this to stand for at least 10 minutes before serving.

STIR in the cooked red quinoa and adjust seasoning with plenty of freshly ground pepper.

DRAIN the mozzarella cheese from any liquid and slice into 1 cm thick pieces.

USING A CAKE RING spoon the quinoa and cabbage salad into the ring then layer the slices of tomato and mozzarella cheese alternatively around the top. Garnish with red endive, baby basil and drizzle with a little olive before serving.

Serves 6

Lemon Chicken Schnitzel Sandwich

A sandwich can be a balanced meal.

2 chicken breast fillets
2 thick slices day-old sourdough bread
2 tablespoons almond meal
2 teaspoons sesame seeds
2 tablespoons pepitas/pumpkin seeds
2 tablespoons plain flour
1 egg, beaten
vegetable oil, for shallow frying

MUSTARD MAYONNAISE
3 teaspoons Dijon mustard
¼ cup low-fat mayonnaise

TO SERVE
fresh sourdough rolls
salad leaves
sliced avocado
sliced tomato

CUT EACH chicken breast in half, slicing through the middle to make two thin fillets. Place between sheets of plastic wrap and pound lightly with a meat mallet to flatten slightly.

REMOVE CRUST from sourdough and process the bread in a food processor until thin crumbs form. Add almond meal, sesame seeds and pepitas and pulse once or twice more. Tip onto a flat plate or tray.

DUST chicken fillets in flour and dip into beaten egg. Crumb in bread/nut mixture. Heat a little oil in a non-stick skillet and cook fillets over medium heat until golden and cooked through. Drain on paper towel to absorb excess oil.

TO MAKE the rolls, mix mayonnaise and mustard together and spread over split rolls. Place avocado and sliced tomato followed by the chicken. Add extra salad to taste.

Serves 4

POWER fOOd Salad

A fantastic source of protein! I often add low-fat fetta to this salad.

1 x 5 oz (150 g) can chickpeas/garbanzo beans
1 x 5 oz (150 g) can three-bean mix
1 large red onion, finely diced
1 green apple
2 large celery sticks
1 carrot
½ lemon, zest and juice
6 egg whites

1 cucumber, diced
9 oz (250 g) fresh podded peas
½ bunch dill, leaves picked
6 oz (180 g) hot smoked salmon, flaked
1 tablespoon pepitas/pumpkin seeds
1 tablespoon sunflower seeds
2 tablespoons olive oil
low-fat fetta cheese, to garnish (optional)

RINSE AND DRAIN chickpeas and mixed beans. Place into a bowl with finely diced red onion.

USING A JUICER, juice the apple, 1 celery stick and 1 carrot. Mix with lemon juice and zest. Pour this juice over the chickpea, bean and onion mix. Cover and refrigerate overnight.

LIGHTLY BEAT the egg whites and pour into a large hot non-stick frying pan. Cook a few minutes each side, then turn the omelette out onto a board and roll up. Allow to cool and slice finely.

STRAIN the chickpeas and bean mixture. Place into a large bowl, retaining the liquid. Finely slice the remaining celery stick and add it to the bean mixture. Stir in the cucumber, peas, dill, salmon, pepitas and sunflower seeds.

WHISK half of the reserved liquid with the olive oil and drizzle over the salad to serve. Crumble fetta over the top if desired.

Serves 4

CHEF'S NOTE: *Hot smoked salmon is available in most good supermarkets and delicatessens. Alternatively, you can use fresh cooked salmon or trout.*

sweet potato fries

Regular potato fries should be off your menu, but if you occasionally feel the urge, these fries are higher in fibre, lower GI and full of nutrients.

20 fl oz (600 ml) vegetable oil
10 oz (300 g) sweet potatoes, peeled
pinch sea salt flakes

IN A DEEP SAUCEPAN heat the oil to 300°F (150°C), making sure the oil does not go over half way up the side of the pan.

CUT THE SWEET POTATOES into long stalks and place carefully into the oil. Keep cooking at 300°F (150°C) for 3 minutes until the fries begin to soften, but do not darken.

CAREFULLY DRAIN and remove from the oil (at this stage you may cool fries and keep in the fridge for later).

TO SERVE, heat the oil to 350°F (175°C) and carefully place the fries back into the oil to cook. They will go golden and crispy (approximately 2–3 minutes). Remove from hot oil and immediately place fries onto paper towels to drain.

ALLOW THE OIL TO COOL, then strain through a fine strainer. Season the hot fries with sea salt flakes and serve.

Serves 4

TWO-bite Chilli beef Sliders

Everyone loves a slider or mini burger. The chillies are spicy but not too hot.

BEEF PATTIES
8 oz (240 g) lean ground/minced beef
1 whole egg
pinch onion powder
sea salt and pepper
2 tablespoons sourdough breadcrumbs
½ teaspoon Worcestershire sauce
½ teaspoon English mustard
½ teaspoon grated horseradish

4 small seeded burger or brioche buns
2 tablespoons low-fat mayonnaise
4 small cob lettuce leaves
2 tablespoons pickled red chillies (see recipe
    page 59

PLACE all beef patty ingredients together in a small bowl and combine.

DIVIDE into four equal parts and shape into small burger patties using a palette knife. Put between 2 small sheets of greaseproof paper and refrigerate until required.

ON A HOT BARBECUE plate or in a non-stick frying pan, cook the burger patties for 2 minutes each side until done to your liking.

SLICE the burger buns in half and toast them lightly. Spread the bottom half with the low-fat mayo. Add a small lettuce leaf to each one, then the burger patties, and spoon over some of the pickled sweet chillies. Insert a small bamboo skewer through the middle of each slider and serve immediately.

Makes 4 sliders

Pickled red Chillies

I enjoy these chilies so much more than the commercial sweet chilli sauce. Use wherever chillies are called. These are a staple in my fridge.

½ teaspoon yellow mustard seeds

1 cup water

3 tablespoons red wine vinegar

1 red onion, finely sliced

1 slice lemon

1 tablespoon superfine/caster sugar

pinch sea salt

8 medium-sized red chillies, finely sliced

1 tablespoon agave syrup

1 tablespoon olive oil

HEAT A SMALL SAUCEPAN over a low heat and toast mustard seeds for 1 minute. Pour in the water, add the red wine vinegar, onion and lemon slice. Bring to the boil and stir in the sugar and the salt.

ADD THE SLICED CHILLIES and bring back to the boil. Remove from the heat immediately. Allow to cool in the saucepan.

ONCE COOL, remove the lemon and drain well. Place chillies into a small bowl, stir through the agave syrup and the olive oil.

Makes approximately 6 serves

Barbecued Salmon San Choy Bau

A great, shared family dish for everyone.

2 teaspoons soy sauce
1 teaspoon agave syrup
2 salmon steaks
pinch ground ginger
1 tablespoon vegetable oil
½ bunch scallions/shallots, sliced
1 red pepper/capsicum, diced

2 tablespoons corn kernels
9 oz (250 g) cooked brown rice
pinch dried chilli flakes (optional)
9 oz (250 g) bean sprouts
1 lemon, juiced
1 large lettuce (iceberg, cob or romaine)

IN A SMALL BOWL, mix together half of the soy sauce and agave syrup and brush over the salmon steaks. Dust them with the ground ginger and place in the fridge for at least 30 minutes or overnight.

WARM OIL in a wok or large non-stick frying pan. Sear the salmon steaks for 2 minutes each side and remove to a plate. After resting for a minute or two, use a fork to flake salmon into small pieces and set aside.

IN THE SAME HOT WOK, add the scallions, red pepper and corn kernels, then stir-fry together for 3 minutes. Add the rice, chilli flakes if using, and a tablespoon of water.

ADD THE SALMON and any juices on the plate and stir-fry together for a one minute. It should be moist but not glugging together. Add bean sprouts. Add a squeeze of fresh lemon juice, season and serve in the leaves of cob, romaine or iceberg lettuce.

Serves 4

Crunchy Chicken nuggets

I love deep-fried chicken and this lower GI version is a fantastic alternative to the fast food options. The buckwheat absorbs less oil than traditional breadcrumbs.

1 lb (500 g) chicken breast, skin removed
12 fl oz (355 ml) buttermilk
3 oz (90 g) whole-wheat flour
sea salt and pepper
pinch paprika
8 oz (240 g) raw buckwheat
4 oz (120 g) almond meal
12 fl oz (355 ml) vegetable or canola oil, for
   frying

DIPPING SAUCE
6 oz (175 g) light sour cream
1 bunch fresh chives, chopped
1 lemon, zest and juice

DICE the chicken breast into 1 in (3 cm) pieces and set aside in the fridge.

POUR THE BUTTERMILK into a small shallow bowl. Place the flour in another small shallow bowl and season with sea salt and a pinch of paprika. Place the raw buckwheat into a mortar and pestle and grind lightly to just crack the kernels. Mix the ground buckwheat and almond meal together and place onto a plate.

COAT the chicken in the flour, dip into the buttermilk and finally coat with buckwheat and almond mixture, making sure each piece is coated well. Roll gently between your palms. Place each crumbed nugget onto a tray lined with a piece of greaseproof paper and chill in the fridge until ready to cook and serve.

MEANWHILE, in a small bowl, combine the sour cream with the chopped fresh chives and the zest and lemon juice.

IN A DEEP SAUCEPAN or deep fryer, heat the oil to 345°F (175°C) and carefully deep-fry the nuggets, for approximately 4 minutes. Remove from the oil onto a paper towel to drain. Serve hot with the sour cream dipping sauce.

Serves 4

3-quinoa salad with broken eggs & iceberg lettuce

This nutty dressing really complements the flavour of the quinoa.

9 oz (250 g) cooked red quinoa
9 oz (250 g) cooked white quinoa
9 oz (250 g) cooked black quinoa
1 tablespoon white vinegar
4 large fresh free range eggs
1 medium-sized iceberg lettuce
1 bunch baby herbs

DRESSING
2 fl oz (60 ml) olive oil
1 tablespoon hazelnut oil
1 teaspoon light soy sauce
juice of ½ lemon
1 teaspoon agave syrup
sea salt and pepper

PLACE all dressing ingredients into a small jar. Place on the lid and shake well until combined.

PLACE each of the different coloured quinoa in its own small bowl and dress each bowl with a third of the dressing. Adjust the seasoning with sea salt and pepper.

BRING A MEDIUM-SIZED saucepan of water to the boil and season with a little salt and a tablespoon of white vinegar. Return the water to a simmer.

POACH THE EGGS in the simmering water for approximately 3 minutes each, leaving them soft.

CUT THE ICEBERG lettuce into large wedges and place on your serving platter. Spoon each of the coloured quinoa around the platter and place the poached eggs on the top. Sprinkle with the cut baby herbs and break the egg yolks using the tip of a small knife just before serving.

Serves 6

Turkey Club Sandwich

This is my favorite sandwich—high in protein and delicious.

1 small red onion, finely chopped
½ clove garlic, crushed
2 avocados, peeled and stone removed
sea salt and pepper
1 lemon
1 tablespoon olive oil
4 rashers bacon
8 thin slices seeded sourdough or
    soy and linseed bread

2 oz (60 g) butter
8 oz (240 g) shaved turkey breast
8 slices reduced fat Swiss-style cheese
4 large eggs
½ iceberg lettuce, finely shredded
2 tablespoons low-fat mayonnaise
sweet potato fries, optional to serve (not included
    in carb exchange)

PREHEAT THE OVEN to 360°F (180°C).

IN A MORTAR AND PESTLE, place the red onion, garlic and avocados and pound to a rough paste, as for a guacamole. Season with sea salt and pepper and a squeeze of lemon juice.

IN A LARGE NON-STICK FRYING PAN heat the oil. Add bacon and cook for 2 minutes. Place on paper towels to drain. Toast 4 slices of bread in a toaster or under a hot grill, spread with butter and place on a baking tray.

SPREAD TOAST with a spoonful of avocado mix then layer on shaved turkey and a rasher of bacon. Top with a cheese slice and place in hot oven.

USING THE SAME PAN and oil the bacon was cooked in, fry the eggs and drain any excess oil, using paper towel. Toast the remaining bread slices.

ONCE THE CHEESE has started melting over the bacon, remove sandwiches from the oven. Place shredded lettuce on the cheese and a dollop of mayonnaise. Place egg on mayonnaise and top with buttered toast. Skewer each side of the sandwich with small wooden skewers and cut into strips or wedges as you like.

SERVE with sweet potato fries and tomato sauce.

Makes 4 large sandwiches

quinoa-crusted fishcakes

The flaked quinoa creates a wonderful crisp crust which is much tastier and less oily than breadcrumbs.

10 oz (300 g) potatoes, peeled and diced
10 oz (300 g) fresh or canned tuna
1 red onion, finely chopped
½ tablespoon fermented chilli bean paste
1 medium red chilli
2 eggs
½ bunch Italian flat-leaf parsley, chopped

2 tablespoons milk
sea salt and pepper
4 oz (120 g) white organic quinoa flakes
3 oz (80 g) all-purpose/plain flour
vegetable oil, for frying

COOK THE POTATOES in boiling salted water until soft. Drain well and mash until smooth, then set aside to cool completely.

DRAIN THE TUNA, then place into a mixing bowl with the diced red onion, chilli bean paste and fresh red chilli. Add the cooled mashed potato, one egg and the chopped parsley. Combine well and adjust the seasoning. The mixture should be firm and dry.

DIVIDE THE FISHCAKE mixture into 8 pieces or 16 small balls and roll in your hands. Place them on a plate and refrigerate for 30 minutes to set.

TO PREPARE for the coating, in a small bowl lightly whisk the remaining egg with the milk and season with a little sea salt and pepper. Place the quinoa flakes and flour into separate bowls.

ROLL THE FISHCAKES firstly in the flour, to lightly coat them. Then dip into the egg mixture and finally press into the quinoa flakes. Shape them into small patties and, using a palette knife, brush off any excess flakes.

PAN-FRY the fishcakes in hot vegetable oil for 2–3 minutes each side until crisp and golden, remove from oil and drain on paper towels.

Makes 8 large or 16 small cakes

Mini fish tacos with soy, avocado & lime

Tacos are the perfect finger food for parties and a great snack to have when you are watching a movie with the family.

4 oz (120 g) fresh kingfish fillet, or other white
  fish fillet
1 small scallion/shallot, finely diced
1 small piece lemongrass, finely chopped
1 medium red chilli, finely chopped
1 lime, zest and juice
½ avocado

sea salt and pepper
1 small knob fresh ginger, grated
½ teaspoon soy sauce
½ bunch fresh cilantro/coriander leaves
8 small crisp taco shells

USING A LARGE KNIFE, finely chop the kingfish and place into a small bowl with the scallion, lemongrass and chilli.

CUT the lime in half. Cut one half into 4 wedges. Zest and juice the other half onto the kingfish.

IN A SEPARATE BOWL mash the avocado with a fork to a smooth paste and season with sea salt and pepper.

ADD THE GINGER, soy sauce and half of the cilantro to the kingfish. Taste and adjust the seasoning.

TO ASSEMBLE, place small taco shells in a stand or between 2 small plates. Spoon in marinated kingfish mixture, top with a teaspoonful of avocado, scatter the remaining cilantro leaves over and serve.

Makes 8 small tacos

Barbecued Whole Shrimp, Cilantro & lime

Fresh, light and tasty, this is such a simple dish. Add extra chilli to your own taste or replace shrimp with fresh grilled salmon or chicken.

3 medium red chillies
1 clove garlic
1 tablespoon agave syrup
juice of 2 limes
12 large fresh shrimp/prawns, with shell on
3 tablespoons olive oil
1 lemon

10 oz (300 g) can organic chickpeas/
 garbanzo beans
1 teaspoon fish sauce
1 bunch fresh cilantro/coriander
½ bunch scallions/spring onions, finely sliced

IN A MORTAR AND PESTLE, pound together the red chilli and garlic to a rough paste. Add agave syrup and the juice of both limes.

PREHEAT a barbecue or grill plate. Brush the shrimps with a little olive oil and place onto the barbecue to cook, with heads and shell on, for approximately 2 minutes each side. Allow them to char and turn a deep red. Meanwhile, cut the lemon in half and place, cut side down, on the barbecue plate.

DRAIN and rinse the chickpeas in a colander. Add the remaining olive oil and fish sauce to the dressing in the mortar and pestle. Stir to combine. Roughly chop the fresh cilantro leaves and add half to the dressing with the sliced scallions.

REMOVE the prawns from the grill and arrange them while still hot onto a serving platter. Place grilled lemons on the side of the platter and spoon the dressing over the hot shrimp.

SPRINKLE with the remaining cilantro leaves and serve.

Serves 4

MAINS

Braised sticky short ribs with steel-cut oats

Oats are not just an ingredient for breakfast, they also make a great side dish.

1 tablespoon olive oil
2 lb (1 kg) short-trimmed beef ribs
2 pints (1.2 litres) beef stock
2 tablespoons agave syrup
9 fl oz (250 ml) balsamic vinegar
1 cinnamon stick
1 lemon, halved

1 small knob butter
½ onion, finely chopped
4 oz (120 g) celeriac, peeled and finely sliced
4 oz (120 g) steel-cut oats
16 fl oz (475 ml) hot vegetable stock
sea salt and pepper

PREHEAT THE OVEN to 360°F (180°C).

IN A HEAVY-BASED SAUCEPAN heat the olive oil and sear the beef ribs on both sides. Remove ribs to an ovenproof dish and allow to rest.

IN A SEPARATE PAN, bring the beef stock to the boil with the agave syrup, balsamic vinegar, cinnamon and lemon. Pour liquid over the beef rib in the ovenproof dish, bring to a rolling boil and cover with a lid. Place the beef into the oven and cook for 1½ hours.

REMOVE beef ribs carefully from the liquid (they should be very soft and tender, almost falling apart), strain the liquid into a clean saucepan and place onto the heat to reduce by two-thirds, until it is a concentrated dark glaze. Brush glaze onto the beef ribs and place them back into the oven for 30 minutes. Continue to brush more glaze on every 10 minutes until ribs become rich and sticky. Keep the ribs warm for serving.

IN A SAUCEPAN, melt the butter and fry the onion and celeriac together for 2 minutes then add the steel-cut oats and gradually stir in the hot vegetable stock. This will thicken quickly, so keep adding the stock until the oats are fully absorbed and soft.

TO SERVE, adjust the seasoning of the oats and brush the hot beef ribs one more time with the glaze.

Serves 4

Angel hair pasta with salmon and chilli lime dressing

4 x 6 oz (180 g) salmon fillet, skin on

sea salt

3 tablespoons olive oil

2 limes, zest and juice

1 tablespoon agave syrup

1 long red chilli, seeds removed and finely
   shredded

2 kaffir lime leaves, finely shredded

3 oz (80 g) angel hair pasta

RUB BOTH SIDES of salmon fillets with a little sea salt and some olive oil. Cook in a heated non-stick frying pan for 1–2 minutes each side, leaving salmon rare.

MIX lime zest, juice, agave, chilli and kaffir lime leaves together, then whisk in the remaining olive oil.

COOK pasta in a large pan of boiling salted water until al dente. Drain well and rinse under cold water. Drain again, place into a bowl and mix through the chilli and lime dressing.

SPOON pasta onto plates and serve with salmon.

Serves 4

Buttermilk shrimp with coconut quinoa

BUTTERMILK SHRIMP
9 oz (250 g) quinoa flakes
10 fl oz (300 ml) buttermilk
12 large fresh green shrimp/prawns,
    peeled and deveined
5 fl oz (150 ml) vegetable oil, for frying
sea salt and pepper

COCONUT QUINOA
9 oz (250 g) cooked white quinoa
6 fl oz (180 ml) light coconut milk
1 tablespoon agave syrup
1 teaspoon fish sauce
1 lime, zest and juice
½ bunch cilantro/coriander leaves
½ fresh Pomelo or ruby grapefruit, segmented

2 kaffir lime leaves, shredded, to serve

IN A MEDIUM-SIZED pot with a lid, place the cooked quinoa, coconut milk and agave syrup and bring to a simmer. Simmer for 5 minutes until all the liquid has been absorbed. Stir with a fork to separate the grains then add the fish sauce, lime zest and juice, and cilantro leaves.

TO MAKE the buttermilk shrimp, place the quinoa flakes onto a small plate and the buttermilk into a small bowl. Pass the shrimp through the buttermilk then coat with the quinoa flakes. Place in the fridge for 10 minutes before frying.

HEAT the oil until hot in a non-stick frying pan then shallow-fry the shrimp for approximately 2 minutes each side, until golden and crisp. Drain on a piece of paper towel and sprinkle with salt and pepper.

TEAR the segments of grapefruit into random pieces and stir through the quinoa.

SPRINKLE with some shredded kaffir lime leaves to serve.

Serves 6

Slow-cooked lamb shanks with Italian vegetables

This combination of flavors works so well together. The cooked meat can also be picked off the bone and served in a sandwich, or flaked over a salad or pasta dish.

4 x 10 oz (300 g) French-trimmed lamb shanks
sea salt and pepper
2 tablespoons olive oil
1 medium onion, finely chopped
1 clove fresh garlic
1 glass red wine
1 sprig fresh rosemary
9 oz (250 g) cherry tomatoes

1 x 12 oz (350 g) can crushed tomatoes
1 medium-sized green zucchini/courgette, thinly sliced
6 oz (175 g) buckwheat, cooked in boiling salted water
12 large green olives
1 bunch fresh sage
selection of seasonal green vegetables

PREHEAT THE OVEN to 360°F (180°C) degrees and heat a large earthenware casserole dish on the stovetop.

SEASON THE LAMB SHANKS with sea salt and pepper. Add the olive oil to the dish and sear the lamb shanks for 3 minutes on all sides.

REMOVE THE SHANKS and add the chopped onion and the garlic to the casserole dish. Cook for 2–3 minutes until softened then add the red wine and the sprig of rosemary. Reduce wine by half, add cherry tomatoes and crushed tomatoes. Return the shanks to the pan and bring to the boil. Cover dish with some foil and a lid and place in the oven for 1½ hours.

AFTER 1 hour 20 minutes, remove from the oven and with a small knife test that the meat is cooked through and falling off the bone. Depending on the actual size of the shanks they may need up to another 30 minutes to cook.

CAREFULLY remove the shanks from the sauce and set aside. Add the sliced green zucchini, buckwheat and green olives to the sauce and stir through. Adjust seasoning with sea salt and pepper.

SPOON the sauce over the shanks and garnish with the fresh sage leaves. Serve with steamed seasonal vegetables.

Serves 4

Angela's veggie lasagne

10 oz (290 g) pumpkin, peeled and sliced
6 large plum tomatoes, halved
½ bunch thyme, leaves picked and chopped
pepper
1 tablespoon extra virgin olive oil
cooking spray
12 dried lasagne sheets

7 oz (210 g) low-fat ricotta (or see recipe
    page 31)
7 oz (210 g) low-fat fetta
½ bunch sage, leaves picked and chopped
zest of 1 lemon
2 tablespoons pepitas/pumpkin seeds

PREHEAT THE OVEN to 350°F (180°C).

PLACE pumpkin and tomatoes into a roasting tray, sprinkle with some of the thyme leaves and pepper, drizzle over oil. Roast in the oven for 25–30 minutes, or until soft. Remove and cool slightly.

GREASE A SMALL LASAGNE DISH with the cooking spray and line the base with sheets of lasagne to fit. (You may need to break some in half.)

SPOON OVER half of the cooked pumpkin and tomato and crumble over a third of the ricotta, fetta and chopped herbs. Repeat with a second layer of lasagne sheets, pumpkin and tomato, cheese and herbs.

TO FINISH, top lasagne with remaining pasta sheets and sprinkle over remaining cheese, herbs, lemon zest and pepitas. Roast in oven for 45–50 minutes. Serve with a spinach, pea and mint salad.

Serves 8

steamed fish fillet with baby spinach & dukkah eggs

The combination of ingredients makes this Angela's personal favorite and most requested dish for me to make at home!

4 x 4 oz (120 g) firm fish fillets (snapper, kingfish)
sea salt and black pepper
2 cups fresh baby spinach
6 large fresh eggs (boiled in shell for 5 minutes)

DUKKAH SPICE MIX
½ cup ground hazelnuts
2 tablespoons sesame seeds
2 tablespoons ground cumin
1 tablespoon ground coriander
1 tablespoon ground fennel seeds
pinch ground nutmeg
pinch ground cloves

PREHEAT THE OVEN to 360°F (180°C). Mix all the dukkah spice ingredients together in a bowl and pour onto a baking sheet. Place in the oven for 6 minutes, mix through with a fork and allow to cool. Keep in an airtight jar for up to 2 weeks.

PLACE a bamboo steamer over a large pan of boiling water (or use an electric steamer if you prefer). Season the snapper fillets with sea salt and freshly ground black pepper and put them onto a small plate, or a piece of greaseproof paper.

PUT THE SPINACH into a small bowl and season with a pinch of sea salt.

PLACE the snapper into the steamer to cook. After 3 minutes place the spinach into the steamer and continue to cook both spinach and snapper for a further 3 minutes until cooked through and firm to touch. Allow fish to rest in the warm steamer.

PEEL the boiled eggs and slice into wedges. Drain any excess water from the spinach. Arrange on a plate with the snapper and wedges of egg. Sprinkle with plenty of the dukkah and serve.

Serves 4

BBQ CHICKEN WITH RED QUINOA TABOULEH SALAD

Fresh and light, this tabouleh salad has many uses

BBQ CHICKEN
1 clove garlic, crushed
1 fl oz (30 ml) olive oil
1 lemon, zest and juice
4 deboned chicken thigh fillets

DRESSING
1 lemon, zest and juice
1 teaspoon tahini paste
2 fl oz (60 ml) olive oil

SALAD
2 bunches flat-leaf parsley, leaves picked and washed, finely chopped
1 bunch fresh mint, leaves picked and washed, finely chopped
1 red onion, finely diced
sea salt and pepper
½ teaspoon sumac (Middle Eastern spice)
1 medium-sized Lebanese cucumber (¼ in/1 cm dice with skin on)
9 oz (250 g) cooked red quinoa
½ cup natural yoghurt

MARINATE THE CHICKEN by mixing together the garlic, olive oil and lemon zest and juice and brushing it onto the chicken thighs. Leave the chicken to marinate for 2 hours.

IN A SMALL BOWL, whisk together the dressing ingredients.

PLACE the chicken thighs onto a hot barbecue or grill plate and cook for approximately 3–4 minutes each side until cooked through. Remove and allow to rest for a few minutes

IN A LARGE SERVING BOWL, combine the parsley, mint and diced red onion. Season with sea salt, pepper and the sumac.

CAREFULLY mix the cucumber and cooked red quinoa through the salad, dressing it as you go.

TO SERVE shred the chicken and place onto the plates. Add a large spoonful of salad and drizzle with a little natural yoghurt.

Serves 4

TUNA, GREEN BEAN, PEANUT AND MINT SALAD

This is a great salad as a main course or even as part of a brunch.

12 oz (360 g) fresh tuna fillet
olive oil
sea salt and pepper
4 oz (120 g) snake beans or green beans,
 finely sliced
2 cups fresh bean shoots
2 small green zucchini/courgette, finely sliced
1 lemon, zest and juice
9 oz (250 g) cooked red quinoa

1 bunch fresh mint, picked leaves

DRESSING
½ cup salted roasted peanuts
1 fl oz (30 ml) olive oil
pinch chilli flakes
2 tablespoons hot water

RUB the fresh tuna fillet with a little olive oil and season with sea salt and pepper.

REHEAT a non-stick frying pan and sear the tuna on each side over a high heat for 1 minute. Allow to cool at room temperature.

IN A SMALL POT of boiling salted water, blanch the sliced green beans for 1 minute then refresh under cold water or in ice. Drain until required.

MAKE THE DRESSING by crushing the peanuts in a mortar and pestle. Stir in the olive oil and chilli flakes. Adjust the thickness with some hot water.

IN A LARGE MIXING BOWL, place the beans, bean shoots and the sliced zucchini. Stir in the lemon zest and juice.

ADD the cooked red quinoa then flake the tuna into the salad. Add the picked mint leaves and dress with the peanut dressing. Mix the salad together carefully, using a spoon.

Serves 4

MOROCCAN-SPICED PUMPKIN, TOMATO AND QUINOA SALAD

This is very filling. Serve it warm or cold with roast lamb or chicken, if you wish.

1 medium-sized kabocha squash/Japanese pumpkin
2 fl oz (60 ml) olive oil
8 Roma tomatoes
1 medium red onion, finely diced
1 clove garlic, crushed
9 oz (250 g) cooked chickpeas/garbanzo beans
9 oz (250 g) cooked black quinoa
9 oz (250 g) cooked red quinoa
sea salt and pepper
1 lime, zest and juice

1 bunch flat-leaf parsley
1 bunch fresh mint
1 bunch fresh coriander/cilantro

SPICE MIX
1 tablespoon fennel seeds
1 tablespoon cumin seeds
1 tablespoon coriander seeds
1 teaspoon flaked sea salt

PREHEAT THE OVEN to 320°F (160°C). Toast the spices in a small non-stick frying pan for 3 minutes. Pour them into a grinder and blend to a powder.

USING A LARGE STRONG KNIFE, cut the pumpkin in half vertically. Scrape out the seeds from the centre and discard. Rub the flesh of one half in a little olive oil and dust with a tablespoon of the spice mix. Place the oiled pumpkin half on a roasting tray with the open side facing up. Bake in the oven for approximately 1 hour 15 minutes until tender. Peel the remaining half of the pumpkin (about 32 oz/900 g) and dice into approximately ¾ in (2 cm) square pieces. Rub these with a little olive oil and place on a roasting tray. Roast for 1 hour until cooked.

CUT the Roma tomatoes in half and rub with some olive oil. Place on a roasting tray and dust with some of the spice mix. Roast in the oven for 45 minutes until cooked and coloured.

IN A LARGE FRYING PAN, heat some olive oil and fry the onion and garlic. After 2 minutes, add the remaining spice mixture and chickpeas. Roughly chop the roasted tomatoes and add to the pan with the diced roasted pumpkin. Stir in the black and red quinoa and cook everything together for 5 minutes. Remove from the heat and allow to cool. Season with sea salt and pepper and stir in the zest and juice of the lime.

TO SERVE, spoon the mixture into the pumpkin half and dress with the picked fresh herbs

Serves 6

PLANK-ROASTED SALMON WITH QUINOA TZATZIKI

1 side or large fillet of salmon
½ clove garlic, crushed
sea salt and pepper
30 ml (1 fl oz) olive oil
½ bunch flat-leaf parsley, roughly chopped
1 lemon, very thinly sliced with skin
1 loaf sourdough bread (not included in carb count) (optional, to serve)

TZATZIKI
1 small cucumber
sea salt and freshly ground black pepper
1 bunch fresh mint
½ clove garlic, crushed
9 fl oz (250 ml) natural Greek-style yoghurt
½ lemon, juice and zest
9 oz (250 g) cooked white quinoa
pinch sumac (Middle Eastern spice)

PREHEAT THE OVEN to 350°F (180°C).

CAREFULLY CHECK all pin bones have been removed from the salmon fillet. Lay the salmon skin-side down onto an untreated cedar plank, rub with the garlic then season with sea salt and plenty of black pepper. Rub with the olive oil. Sprinkle the parsley onto the salmon and cover with the thin slices of lemon.

PLACE THE SALMON on the plank into the oven for 8–12 minutes or until cooked how you like it.

TO MAKE THE TZATZIKI, cut the cucumber in half, scrape out the seeds then grate the cucumber, with the skin on. Place this into a small bowl and season with sea salt. Leave it to stand for 30 minutes then drain all the liquid away.

WITH A SHARP KNIFE, finely shred the mint leaves and mix with the cucumber, crushed garlic and yoghurt in a large bowl. Season with the zest and juice of the lemon and freshly ground black pepper. Stir in the quinoa and sumac and mix well.

SERVE the bowl of tzatziki with the warm salmon on the board with some hot fresh bread.

CHEF'S NOTE: *Make sure that you use untreated cedar for your plank. You can purchase this from your local hardware store and cut it to size to fit in your oven. It will burn or smoke a little in the oven but that's fine—the smoke will impart a beautiful flavor to the salmon.*

Serves 6

High protein spaghetti bolognese

I always try to have a higher percentage of meat, but you can adjust to your liking or even make this with tofu.

2½ tablespoons olive oil

8 oz (240 g) beef scotch fillet, diced ¼ in (½ cm)

8 oz (240 g) pork loin fillet diced ¼ in (½ cm)

1 onion, chopped

1 clove garlic

a splash of red wine

4 oz (120 g) Roma tomatoes, diced

9 oz (250 g) cherry tomatoes

1 x 14 oz (400 g) crushed tomatoes

1 pint (600 ml) vegetable stock

1 sprig lemon thyme

4 oz (120 g) tofu, fried and diced ¼ in (½ cm)

sea salt and black pepper

dried chilli flakes (optional)

3 slices soy and linseed bread

3 oz (80 g) grated parmesan cheese

8 oz (240 g) whole-wheat or gluten-free spaghetti

PREHEAT THE OVEN to 360°F (180°C).

HEAT A LARGE FRYING pan or casserole dish over a medium heat. Add half the olive oil and fry together the seasoned diced beef and pork loin together. Sauté for 3 minutes, then add the onion and garlic. Cook for another 2 minutes. Add a splash of red wine and reduce the sauce by half. Add all of the tomatoes and the vegetable stock.

DROP IN the lemon thyme, cover with a lid and simmer for 45 minutes. Check that the meat is tender using a small knife. Add the diced tofu. Adjust the seasoning with salt and pepper or add dried chilli if you prefer. Reduce the sauce to a thick texture.

TOAST the soy and linseed bread and put into a blender with the parmesan cheese. Pulse together for 1 minute until you have a coarse crumb. Add a tablespoon of olive oil, pour the oiled crumbs onto a lined baking tray and bake in the oven for 3 minutes.

COOK THE SPAGHETTI in boiling salted water as per packet directions, until al dente. Drain and place spaghetti in a large bowl in the middle of the table with the rich sauce on the top and sprinkle with the parmesan crumbs.

Serves 4

SIOW-COOKed TUrKey with ricotta and spinach

This stuffing keeps the top breast meat nice and moist!

4 oz (120 g) spinach leaves
6 oz (180 g) low-fat ricotta (or see recipe
   page 31)
1 lemon, zest and juice
1 clove garlic, crushed
salt and pepper
1 tablespoon olive oil

10 lb (3 kg) whole turkey

PREHEAT THE OVEN to 300°F (150°C).

BLANCH spinach in boiling salted water for 1 minute and refresh under cold water. Squeeze as dry as possible. Roughly chop spinach.

MIX ricotta in a bowl until smooth. Add the spinach, lemon juice and zest, garlic and season with salt and pepper.

FORCE your fingers between the skin and breast meat. Spoon the ricotta mix into this area, spreading out evenly. Rub the turkey with a little olive oil. Place in a deep roasting pan.

ROAST in the oven for 2 hours. Remove and rest for 15 minutes in a warm place before carving.

SERVE sliced turkey with roasted vegetables.

Serves 6–8

warm seafood and quinoa salad

9 oz (250 g) quinoa

8 oz (240 g) sea bass fillet

8 oz (240 g) salmon fillet, skin off

8 oz (240 g) peeled medium raw shrimp/prawns

5 oz (150 g) scallops

splash of extra virgin olive oil

salt and pepper

3½ oz (100 g) green beans, blanched and
  refreshed in cold water

1 x 4 oz (120 g) can red kidney beans, rinsed
  and drained

DRESSING

1 large clove garlic, finely grated

2 sprigs rosemary, leaves picked and finely
  chopped

2–3 anchovy fillets, finely chopped

3½ fl oz (100 ml) extra virgin olive oil

1 lemon, zest and juice

sea salt and pepper

RINSE QUINOA several times in cold water and drain. Cook in a saucepan of boiling salted water for 15 minutes. Drain and rinse again. Set aside.

PLACE THE SEAFOOD onto a baking tray and brush with a little oil. Season with salt and pepper. Grill (broil) for 4–8 minutes or until seafood is just cooked.

MAKE THE DRESSING in a mortar and pestle by pounding together the garlic, rosemary and anchovy fillets until broken down. Add the oil, lemon zest and juice. Mix well and adjust the seasoning to taste.

STIR THE DRESSING into the quinoa, green beans and kidney beans. Spoon the salad over the warm seafood to serve.

Serves 4

Pumpkin-crusted fish on mash

10½ oz (300 g) pumpkin, peeled and cut into
  cubes
1 orange, quartered with peel left on
sea salt and pepper
9 fl oz (250 ml) non-fat natural yoghurt
¼ bunch basil, leaves picked and shredded
½ cup raw pepitas/pumpkin seeds

4 x 5 oz (160 g) sea bass fillets (or equivalent
  firm flesh fish)
cooking spray

PREHEAT THE OVEN to 350°F (180°C).

PLACE PUMPKIN and orange into a roasting dish and roast in the oven for 45 minutes, or until pumpkin is cooked. Remove half of the orange and set aside.

SQUEEZE removed orange segments into the pumpkin and mash coarsely with a fork. Season with salt and pepper and set aside to keep warm.

SQUEEZE juice from remaining orange segments into yoghurt and stir in basil. Season to taste.

CRUSH PEPITAS in a mortar and pestle until they have the consistency of coarse breadcrumbs.

SEASON THE FISH and press each fillet into the pepitas, ensuring it is evenly covered. Spray lightly with cooking spray and cook in a hot non-stick frying pan for 2–3 minutes each side.

SERVE the fish on the warm pumpkin mash with a spoonful of the orange and basil yoghurt. Serve with a large green salad on the side.

Serves 4

A healthy meal on a pizza

This dish can easily be changed to suit your taste. Simply add grilled chicken, sliced steak or grilled shrimp.

BASE

1 large pita or Lebanese bread

½ cup napolitana sauce

3 oz (80 g) button mushrooms, finely sliced

1 medium-sliced green zucchini/courgette, finely sliced

2 eschallots/French shallots or 1 red onion

4 oz (120 g) small bocconcini cheese

4 oz (120 g) grape or cherry tomatoes

½ bunch fresh parsley

½ cup low-fat mozzarella, grated

TOPPING

2 cups baby spinach or arugula/rocket leaves

2 ripe avocados, peeled, stone removed and diced

3 oz (80 g) low-fat fetta cheese, crumbled

4 bacon rashers, grilled

4 oz (120 g) grape or cherry tomatoes

4 red radishes, finely sliced

½ cup fresh herbs

sea salt and pepper

2 tablespoons olive oil

1 lemon

PREHEAT THE OVEN to 360°F (180°C).

PLACE THE BREAD on a large baking tray, spread a little of the Napolitana sauce over and then, in a random fashion, sprinkle the sliced mushrooms, zucchini and eschallots over the top. Chop the bocconcini, grape tomatoes and parsley and scatter them randomly over the bread. Sprinkle with the grated mozzarella and season with sea salt and pepper. Bake in the oven for 12 minutes.

PLACE the spinach leaves into a mixing bowl and mix with the remaining topping ingredients, except the oil and lemon, like a mixed salad. Season well and dress with the olive oil and a squeeze of lemon.

REMOVE the hot bread from the oven and allow to cool for 2 minutes. Spoon the salad topping onto the bread. Cut into large wedges, season and serve.

Serves 6

Polenta-crusted pork with fennel & orange salad

4 pork cutlets, trimmed of extra fat
9 oz (250 g) coarse polenta
cooking spray
1 large fennel bulb, trimmed
2 oranges, peeled and segmented
½ bunch flat-leaf parsley, leaves picked
sea salt and pepper

DATE HONEY SAUCE
4 dates, pitted and chopped
juice of ¼ lemon
2 fl oz (60 ml) water
1 fl oz (30 ml) agave syrup

TO MAKE THE DATE HONEY SAUCE, mash the dates lightly with a fork. Place into a small saucepan with the lemon juice, water and agave. Cook, stirring over a low heat, until the water has been absorbed and it has a thick consistency. Cool completely.

PRESS PORK cutlets into the polenta to coat evenly. Spray cutlets with cooking spray and cook in a non-stick skillet (frying pan) over medium high heat until cooked through. Remove and rest for 5 minutes.

SHAVE FENNEL on a cutter into very thin slices. Mix with orange segments and any juices. Add picked parsley.

MIX DATE HONEY SAUCE roughly and toss through salad. Season with salt and pepper.

SERVE cutlets with salad.

Serves 4

crusted beef with sticky sweet potato & mustard cream

One of my favourite Sunday lunches.

STICKY SWEET POTATO
1 lb 9 oz (700 g) sweet potato
1 tablespoon agave syrup
2 tablespoons light soy sauce

16 oz (480 g) beef tenderloin
cooking spray
3 oz (90 g) sunflower seeds
3 oz (90 g) whole almonds
3 oz (90 g) walnuts
2 oz (60 g) low-fat spread or butter

MUSTARD AND HORSERADISH CREAM
2 tablespoons horseradish puree or sauce
2 tablespoons wholegrain mustard
1 clove garlic, crushed
1 eschalot/French shallot, finely chopped
¼ bunch parsley, finely chopped
3 oz (90 g) light sour cream
sea salt and freshly ground black pepper

PREHEAT THE OVEN to 400°F (200°C).

PEEL AND CUT sweet potato into large chunks. Coat well with agave and soy sauce and place onto a shallow baking sheet. Roast in the oven for 35 minutes, turning over halfway through the cooking time.

SPRAY TENDERLOIN with cooking spray and seal evenly in a hot non-stick frying pan for 2 minutes each side, or until brown. Remove and cool.

PROCESS SEEDS and nuts to a coarse crumb. Add butter and process until just mixed through. Press nut crust onto beef tenderloin and reduce heat to a moderate oven (350°F/180°C) and bake for 25 minutes. Set aside to rest for 10 minutes before slicing.

MIX MUSTARD and horseradish ingredients together and season to taste.

SERVE SLICED beef with sweet potato and mustard and horseradish cream.

Serves 6

DESSERTS

Not-so-naughty chocolate cake

A low-fat, low GI, high protein, low sugar chocolate cake.

10 oz (300 g) fresh full cream ricotta cheese (or
   see recipe page 31)
1 oz (30 g) unsweetened pure cocoa powder
4 fl oz (120 ml) fresh milk (2% fat)
2 tablespoons agave syrup
2 oz (60 g) butter
6 oz (175 g) self-rising/self-raising flour
½ teaspoon baking soda/bicarbonate of soda
2 oz (60 g) almond meal
3 large fresh eggs

CHOCOLATE TOPPING
4 fl oz (120 ml) light cream
2 drops vanilla essence
1 teaspoon agave syrup
4 oz (120 g) dark chocolate, 71% cocoa, chopped

TO SERVE
4 fl oz (120 ml) cream, lightly whisked with
   1 teaspoon agave syrup
fresh berries or figs
dark chocolate shavings
confectioners'/icing sugar

PREHEAT THE OVEN to 360°F (180°C). In a large mixing bowl or electric kitchen mixer, beat the ricotta vigorously for 3 minutes until very smooth.

MIX THE COCOA into a small amount of the milk, then pour into a small saucepan with the remaining milk and agave syrup and warm over a low heat. Stir in the butter to melt then allow to cool. Sift the flour, baking soda and ground almonds onto a sheet of greaseproof paper to aereate the flour.

IN A SEPARATE BOWL, lightly whisk eggs with a fork. With the mixer on a medium speed, gradually add the egg to the ricotta then add the milk and butter mixture. Add the flour and almond mix and beat to combine. Do not over-mix at this point.

GREASE AND LINE a 8 in (20 cm) cake tin with greaseproof paper. Pour mix into tin and bake in oven for 30 minutes—do not open oven during cooking. Invert cake on to a cooling wire rack and allow to cool.

TO MAKE THE CHOCOLATE TOPPING, warm the cream, vanilla and agave syrup in a small pan. Remove from heat and add the chocolate. Stir until mixed and allow to cool. Do not refrigerate.

USING A LARGE BREAD KNIFE, slice the cake into three pieces horizontally. Then spread each layer with some of the chocolate topping, the whisked cream and the fresh fruit. Finally garnish the top with some dark chocolate shavings and a very light dusting of confectioners' sugar.

Makes one large 3-layered cake | Serves 12

peanut butter & chocolate mini tartlets

½ packet filo pastry
2 oz (60 g) butter, melted
1 tablespoon agave syrup
6 fl oz (175 ml) light cream
½ teaspoon vanilla essence
4 oz (120 g) dark chocolate buttons
   (71% chocolate)

3 oz (80 g) low-fat crunchy peanut butter
1 tablespoon dark cocoa powder
fresh raspberries or strawberries to garnish

PREHEAT OVEN to 360°F (180°C). Brush a sheet of filo pastry with melted butter and place another sheet of filo on top. Repeat with two other layers. Cut layered filo using a pastry ring to fit the size of small tartlet moulds, approximately 1 in (3 cm) in diameter. Line the moulds with the filo and some baking parchment discs, then place some rice or beans inside, to act as pastry weights.

BLIND BAKE PASTRY in the oven for 3 minutes, remove from oven and discard the pastry weights and parchment. Return pastry shells to the oven and bake for a further 3 minutes until golden and crisp. Remove from the oven and allow to cool.

IN A SMALL SAUCEPAN, bring the agave and the cream to the boil with the vanilla essence. Place chocolate buttons into a bowl and pour over hot cream mix. Stir together until smooth. Set aside and allow to cool, but do not refrigerate.

IF CHOCOLATE HASN'T MELTED enough, microwave it briefly.

TO MAKE THE TARTLETS, place some peanut butter in the bottom of each one and pipe or spoon the chocolate mixture on the top. Dust with a little dark cocoa and finish with a raspberry or a strawberry.

Makes approximately 20 small tartlets | 2 per portion

UPSIDE-DOWN APPLE & PEAR CRUNCH

3 oz (90 g) unsalted butter

2 fl oz (60 ml) agave syrup

1 teaspoon ground nutmeg

1 teaspoon ground ginger

1 teaspoon ground cinnamon

4 green apples, peeled, cored and cut into wedges

2 green pears, peeled, washed and cut into wedges

CRUNCH TOPPING

1 oz (30 g) unsalted butter

2 tablespoons agave syrup

2 tablespoons rolled barley oats

½ cup cooked red quinoa

2 tablespoons almond meal

2 tablespoons sunflower seeds

2 tablespoons pepita/pumpkin seeds

2 tablespoons flax seeds

1 tablespoon pecan nuts, roughly chopped

PREHEAT THE OVEN to 360°F (180°C).

IN A NON-STICK FRYING PAN, melt the butter, agave and spices together. Add the wedges of apple and pear and cook on a low heat for 45 minutes until the fruit is soft and caramelised.

IN A SMALL BOWL, melt together the butter and agave for the crunch topping.

IN A MIXING BOWL, combine the rest of the ingredients of the crunch topping and coat everything in the melted agave and butter mix.

LINE A SMALL PIE DISH with a piece of greased paper then pack the fruit in firmly. Sprinkle over the crunch topping then bake in the oven for 35 minutes.

REMOVE from the oven and allow to cool for 5 minutes before serving. Then carefully invert onto your serving plate.

Serves 8

CHEF'S NOTE: *Serve with a little light pouring cream or some agave ice cream.*

Roast peaches with zabaglione & sunflower seeds

Late summer peaches are best.

4 peaches or nectarines, stoned and halved
2 tablespoons sunflower seeds
1 tablespoon agave syrup
2 eggs, plus 2 extra yolks
2 fl oz (60 ml) peach nectar juice
confectioners'/icing sugar, to dust

PREHEAT THE OVEN to 350°F (180°C).

PLACE PEACHES, cut side up, into a roasting dish and dust lightly with icing sugar. Sprinkle sunflower seeds on the top and bake in oven for 20 minutes.

TO MAKE THE ZABAGLIONE, whisk agave, eggs and yolks together in a bowl over a pan of simmering water, while gradually adding the nectar. Continue to whisk until the mixture is thick, frothy and pale yellow in colour; do not let it get too hot.

SERVE WARM PEACHES in a small bowl or glass drizzled with zabaglione.

Serves 4

citrus & poppy seed cake

CAKE MIXTURE

2 lemons

3 large oranges

3 cups water

3 tablespoons agave syrup

2 cardamom pods

1 oz (30 g) butter

3 eggs, lightly beaten

8 oz (240 g) almond meal

2 tablespoons whey protein powder

1 teaspoon baking soda/bicarbonate of soda

2 tablespoons poppy seeds

2 tablespoons self-rising/self-raising flour

cooking spray

SYRUP

2 tablespoons freshly squeezed orange juice

juice of ¼ lemon

1 tablespoon agave syrup

PREHEAT THE OVEN to 360°F (180°C).

PEEL LEMONS AND ORANGES, discard rind, and slice fruit approximately ¼ in (½ cm) thick.

PLACE FRUIT in a medium-sized saucepan with the water, agave syrup and cardamom pods. Cover with a lid and place on a medium heat to simmer for approximately 2 hours until the fruit is totally cooked and broken down, and has a marmalade-like consistency. Take care not to burn as it will become very sticky as it nears the end of its cooking.

REMOVE THE CARDAMOM pods and discard. Stir in the butter to melt and allow mixture to cool. Place fruit mixture into a mixing bowl and stir in the lightly beaten eggs. Stir in the almond meal, protein powder, baking soda, poppy seeds and the flour. Mix well together. It will be quite loose at this point.

LINE AN 8 IN (20 cm) cake tin with greaseproof paper and a spray of oil. Pour in the cake mixture and bake for 25 minutes until golden and firm to touch. Meanwhile, to make the syrup, warm the orange and lemon juice with the agave.

ONCE COOKED, remove the cake from the oven and allow to cool on a cooling wire. Turn it over and place onto your serving plate, brush it with the warm syrup and allow it to soak in.

Serves 12

toffee, carrot, honey & nut slice

12 oz (350 g) fresh full-cream ricotta cheese (or
  see recipe page 31)
2 tablespoons agave syrup
4 fl oz (120 ml) fresh milk (2% fat)
2 oz (60 g) butter
1 tablespoon vegetable oil
6 oz (175 g) self-rising/self-raising flour
½ teaspoon baking soda/bicarbonate of soda
2 oz (60 g) almond meal

3 large fresh eggs
6 oz (175 g) fresh carrot, grated
2 oz (60 g) walnuts, roughly chopped
2 oz (60 g) slithered almonds
2 oz (60 g) pistachio nuts, chopped
4 oz (120 g) crème fraîche for frosting,
  sweetened with a little agave syrup
cinnamon or confectioners'/icing sugar to dust

PREHEAT THE OVEN to 360°F (180°C). Using an electric mixer, beat the ricotta for 3 minutes on a high speed until very smooth.

IN A SMALL SAUCEPAN melt the agave syrup with the milk, butter and oil then allow to cool.

IN A BOWL, sift together the flour, baking soda and the ground almonds.

REDUCE THE MIXER SPEED to slow, then gradually add the eggs and the milk mixture. Add the flour mixture combine everything together, but do not over-mix.

STIR IN the grated carrot, walnuts, almonds and the pistachio nuts and mix through.

GREASE AND LINE a large toffee tray with greaseproof paper and spread the mixture evenly into it. Bake in the oven for 30 minutes until firm to touch. Remove from the oven and allow to cool in the tray. Using a large knife, score the cake into portions approximately 2 in (5 cm) square or to your liking. Spread some crème fraîche on the top or dust with cinnamon or a little confectioners' sugar.

Makes 1 large tray | approximately 12 serves

BAKED STRAWBERRY, LIME & QUINOA CUSTARD PUDDING

3 large fresh free range eggs

2 fl oz (60 ml) agave syrup

1 teaspoon vanilla paste

½ lime, zest and juice

2 tablespoons quinoa flour

9 oz (250 g) cooked white quinoa

9 fl oz (250 ml) cream

9 fl oz (250 ml) milk

1 lb (500 g) large fresh strawberries

PREHEAT THE OVEN to 350°F (180°C).

USING AN ELECTRIC BEATER, whisk together the eggs with the agave syrup, vanilla paste and the lime zest and juice.

WHISK in the quinoa flour until combined then stir in the cooked white quinoa.

IN A SMALL PAN, bring the cream and milk to a simmer then remove from the heat and allow to cool for 5 minutes.

STIRRING CONSTANTLY, pour the cream mixture over the egg mixture.

TRIM the tops from the strawberries and arrange in a small baking pie dish with the tips facing up.

CAREFULLY pour the quinoa custard around the strawberries, leaving the tips uncovered.

BAKE in a preheated oven for 1 hour until custard is set and light brown in colour.

SERVE WARM with some pouring cream or ice cream.

Serves 8

Index

ABOUT THE AUTHOR

With a career in food spanning almost three decades, Michael Moore is no ordinary chef, he is better described as a global entrepreneur.

With a passion for nutrition and a fervent interest in the science behind food, the popular television chef and author is able to make high-end food preparation both accessible to the home cook and desired by the discerning restaurant patron.

Michael is renowned across three continents for his work as a chef as well as his food consultancy, cookbooks and personal appearances.

Michael has owned and managed numerous top restaurants in both London and Sydney including the Ritz Hotel London, Kables, Craigend, Hotel Nikko, the Bluebird London, Bennelong, Prunier's, Bonne Femme and Wildfire. He has earned critical praise on both sides of the globe, as well as a number of coveted media awards.

Michael is currently the chef and owner of O Bar and Dining in Sydney. *Blood Sugar: Quinoa & Healthy Living* is Michael's fourth book, and follows *Moore to Food*, *Blood Sugar* and *Blood Sugar: The Family*.

www.michaelmoorechef.com
www.obardining.com.au
twitter: @michaelmooresyd
facebook: /chefmichaelmoore

Weights and Measures

½ metric teaspoon	2.5ml
1 metric teaspoon	5ml
2 teaspoons	10ml
1 tablespoon	20ml

CUPS
All measures are based on level cupfuls.

LIQUID

1 cup	250ml (9fl oz)
½ cup	125ml (4fl oz)

SOLIDS

1 cup flour	120g (4oz)
1 cup white sugar	180g (6oz)
1 cup light brown sugar	120g (4oz)
1 cup caster sugar	120g (4oz)
1 cup chopped nuts	180g (6oz)
1 cup grated cheese	90g (3oz)

OVEN TEMPERATURES

100°C	very slow	200°F	Gas Mark 1
120°C	very slow	250°F	Gas Mark 1
150°C	slow	300°F	Gas Mark 2
160°C	warm	325°F	Gas Mark 2–3
180°C	moderate	350°F	Gas Mark 4
190°C	moderately hot	375°F	Gas Mark 5
200°C	moderately hot	400°F	Gas Mark 6
220°C	hot	420°F	Gas Mark 7
230°C	very hot	450°F	Gas Mark 8
250°C	very hot	485°F	Gas Mark 9

First published in 2013 by
New Holland Publishers
London • Sydney • Cape Town • Auckland
www.newhollandpublishers.com

The Chandlery Unit 114 50 Westminster Bridge Road London SE1 7QY
1/66 Gibbes Street Chatswood NSW 2067 Australia
Wembley Square First Floor Solan Road Gardens Cape Town 8001 South Africa
218 Lake Road Northcote Auckland New Zealand

A catalogue record of this book is available at the British Library and at the National Library of Australia

ISBN: 9781742574561

10 9 8 7 6 5 4 3 2 1

Publisher: Fiona Schultz
Project editor: Jodi De Vantier
Designer: Tracy Loughlin
Recipes and food styling: Michael Moore
Photographer: Steve Brown
Production director: Olga Dementiev
Printer: Toppan Leefung Printing Limited

Follow New Holland Publishers on
Facebook: www.facebook.com/NewHollandPublishers